GIANT OCEAN ANIMALS

I0875955

BLUE WHALE

Massive Mammal

BY EMMANUEL MARSHALL

Enslow PUBLISHING

Please visit our website, www.enslow.com. For a free color catalog of all our high-quality books, call toll free 1-800-398-2504 or fax 1-877-980-4454.

Cataloging-in-Publication Data
Names: Marshall, Emmanuel.
Title: Blue whale / Emmanuel Marshall.
Description: Buffalo, NY : Enslow Publishing, 2027. | Series: Giant ocean animals | Includes glossary and index.
Identifiers: ISBN 9781978550599 (pbk.) | ISBN 9781978550605 (library bound) | ISBN 9781978550612 (ebook)
Subjects: LCSH: Blue whale--Juvenile literature.
Classification: LCC QL737.C424 M377 2027 | DDC 599.5248--dc23

Published in 2027 by
Enslow Publishing
2544 Clinton Street
Buffalo, NY 14224

Copyright © 2027 Enslow Publishing

Portions of this work were originally authored by Katie Chanez and published as *Blue Whales*. All new material in this edition was authored by Emmanuel Marshall.

Cover Designer: Joshua Olson
Interior Designer: Joshua Olson
Editor: Noah Riccardi

Photo Credits: Cover, p. 1 Ajit S. N./Shutterstock.com; pp. 4–5 Andrew Sutton/Shutterstock.com; pp. 6–7 Rich Carey/Shutterstock.com; pp. 8–9, 14–15 NOAA; pp. 10–11 Sophie Webb/NOAA/Point Blue; pp. 12–13 Jo Crebbin/Shutterstock.com; pp. 16–17 Treap News/Shutterstock.com; pp. 18–19 Wirestock Creators/Shutterstock.com; pp. 20–21 Lpettet/iStockphoto; pp. 22–23, 29 Romana Kontowiczova/Shutterstock.com; p. 24 ra66/Shutterstock.com; p. 25 Evren Kalinbacak/Shutterstock.com; pp. 26–27 cybercrisi/Shutterstock.com.

All rights reserved. No part of this book may be reproduced in any form without permission in writing from the publisher, except by a reviewer.

Printed in China

Some of the images in this book illustrate individuals who are models. The depictions do not imply actual situations or events.

CPSIA compliance information: Batch #QS27ENS: For further information contact Enslow Publishing, at 1-800-398-2504.

Find us on

TABLE OF CONTENTS

CHAPTER 1

GIANT SWIMMERS

Blue whales are giant **mammals**. They live in oceans all over the world. Some blue whales **migrate** to warmer waters in the winter. Some live in the same place all year long.

The west coast of the United States is a good place to spot blue whales.

Most blue whales are 70 to 90 feet (21–27 m) long. Some grow even bigger.

Blue whales are the largest animals on Earth. They can be longer than 100 feet (30 m) long. That's longer than a basketball court.

A blue whale can weigh more than 18 school buses!

A whale breathes air through a blowhole on the top of its head.

Blue whales breathe air. They come to the surface to breathe. Then they go back under. They can go an hour between breaths.

SWIM SPEEDS

Blue whales can swim up to 20 miles per hour (32 km/h). But they can't go that fast for long. They usually swim about 5 miles per hour (8 km/h).

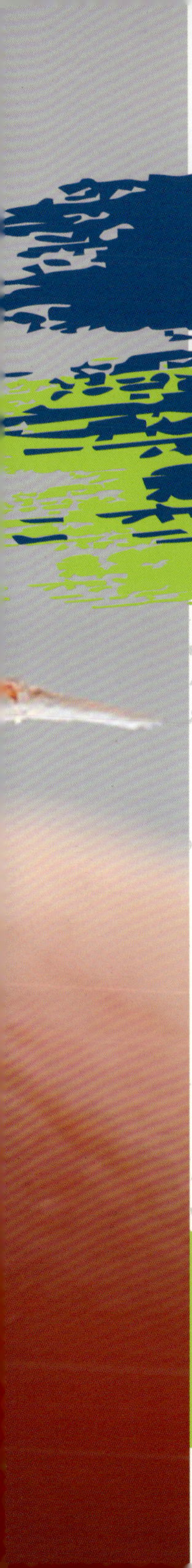

CHAPTER 2

LIFE IN THE WILD

Blue whales eat **krill**. Whales catch these small creatures in their large mouths. They open their mouths while swimming forward. Water rushes into the whales' mouths. So do krill.

Some types of krill can fit on a person's fingertip.

Whales use their tongues to push the water out. But the krill get trapped in the whales' **baleen**. The whales swallow the krill.

A blue whale's mouth could fit 100 people inside of it.

The gray whale is another kind of whale with baleen.

BALEEN

Many types of whales have thin **plates** in their mouths. The plates are called baleen. They let water through. But the plates trap small animals such as krill.

In the summer, blue whales often swim to places where they can find food.

Most blue whales live alone. But sometimes they swim in pairs. Other times, they swim in small groups.

The largest blue whales live near Antarctica.

A baby blue whale is called a calf. A mother whale gives birth to a calf. The calf **nurses** for about seven months. Then it is ready to live on its own.

A whale pair often includes a mother and baby.

Scientists measure a blue whale's age by studying its earwax.

CHAPTER 3

WHALE CALLS

Blue whales **communicate** with one another. They use moans, groans, and other calls. These calls can travel many miles.

Whales from different parts of the world have different calls.

Some scientists research whale calls. They are learning what different calls mean. For example, whales might use calls to find other whales. And different groups of whales might have different sounds.

NOISY WATERS

More boats are in the ocean today than 100 years ago. Boat noise can cause problems for whales. It can stop whales from hearing one another. It can also change how they swim.

When blue whales are migrating, they sing more during the day. When they stay put, they sing more at night.

CHAPTER 4

SAVING WHALES

Blue whales are **endangered**. That's mainly because of humans. In the past, many people hunted whales. As few as 10,000 blue whales may be left.

Blue whales can dive up to 1,640 feet (500 m) underwater.

Hunting whales is now against the law. But people can still harm whales by **accident**. Boats sometimes hit them. Blue whales can also get caught in fishing nets.

Many people travel on boats to see whales.

Many blue whales are hurt or killed when large ships crash into them.

KRILL FISHING

People fish for krill. Krill can be used to make animal food. But taking krill from the ocean leaves less food for whales to eat.

People are learning how to stop whales from getting stuck in fishing nets.

Blue whales can live to be more than 80 years old.

People are trying to stop these harmful things from happening. As a result, blue whales' numbers are beginning to grow.

TEST YOUR KNOWLEDGE

Take this quiz to test your knowledge.

1. Write a sentence that describes the key ideas from Chapter 4.
2. Would you ever want to swim with a blue whale? Why or why not?
3. How long can blue whales be?
   A. less than 10 feet (3 m)
   B. about 40 feet (12 m)
   C. more than 100 feet (30 m)
4. How did blue whales become endangered?
   A. Sharks attacked too many blue whales.
   B. People fed blue whales too much food.
   C. People hunted too many blue whales.

5. What does **research** mean in this book?

*Some scientists **research** whale calls. They are learning what different calls mean.*

A. to lose
B. to study
C. to stay away from

6. What does **moans** mean in this book?

*They use **moans**, groans, and other calls. These calls can travel many miles.*

A. big, round eyes
B. loud, low sounds
C. short, thick fur

Answers can be found on page 32.

GLOSSARY

accident
Not on purpose.

baleen
Plates that some whales have instead of teeth. They help whales catch food.

communicate
To send and receive messages.

endangered
In danger of dying out forever.

krill
Small animals that float in the sea. They look like shrimp.

mammals
Animals that have hair and produce milk for their young.

migrate
To move from one part of the world to another.

nurses
Drinks milk from its mother.

plates
Things that are smooth, flat, and thin.

FOR MORE INFORMATION

BOOKS

Fenmore, Taylor. *Blue Whales: Nature's Biggest Mammal.* Minneapolis, MN: Lerner Publications, 2024.

Humphrey, Natalie. *Blue Whale: Massive Mammal.* Buffalo, NY: Rosen Publishing, 2024.

WEBSITES

National Geographic Kids: Blue Whale

kids.nationalgeographic.com/animals/mammals/facts/blue-whale

Find out more about Earth's largest animal.

PBS LearningMedia: Guess How Whales Hear!

thinktv.pbslearningmedia.org/resource/tdc02.sci.life.colt.ologist/guess-how-whales-hear/

Find out how blue whales can hear underwater.

Publisher's note to educators and parents: Our editors have carefully reviewed these websites to ensure that they are suitable for students. Many websites change frequently, however, and we cannot guarantee that a site's future contents will continue to meet our high standards of quality and educational value. Be advised that students should be closely supervised whenever they access the internet.

INDEX

Answer Key:
1. Answers will vary; 2. Answers will vary; 3. C; 4. C; 5. B; 6. B